Printed in China

This Girl Walks Into A Bar
ISBN 978-0692387382

COCKTAILS FOR

Cougars

AND COWGIRLS

SIMPLE AND DELICIOUS RECIPES

for Every Woman

BY

JORDAN CATAPANO

Designed by Jocelyn Dunn Muhlbach

Jordan Catapano

Welcome!

This recipe book is dedicated to you!

The cougars and the cowgirls, the executives and the homemakers, the young brides and the grandmothers who have all contributed to the identity of our company — you are the inspiration for this collection of cocktails. We'd like to think that there's a little bit of each of these women in all of us.

This book has been a genuine labor of love over the past few years. Between running our business and raising our families, we've somehow managed to find a moment here or there to test a recipe, get it just right, photograph it, and then of course, put it all together in a book. Seeing this project through often meant getting up before the break of dawn and staying up late enough to "hear" the silence in the house. But when there's a driving force like our loyal blog and book readers to complete a project, it's easy to find the motivation to see it through to the end.

RED VELVET

Ingredients

1 ounce gin
4 ounces prosecco
¾ ounce crème de cassis
½ ounce sweet vermouth
¼ ounce lemon juice
Lemon garnish

Batch Recipe (serves 8-10)

6 ounces gin
1 bottle prosecco
6 ounces crème de cassis
6 ounces sweet vermouth
3 ounces lemon juice
Lemon garnish

Directions

Combine the gin, crème de cassis, lemon juice, and sweet vermouth in the glass. Gently swirl or stir to mix. Tilt the glass to a 45° angle and slowly add the prosecco. Garnish with lemons and serve.

GLASSWARE: Champagne flute, wine glass, stemless wine glass

JUST PEACHY

Ingredients

5 ounces Champagne
2 ½ ounces orange juice
½ ounce peach schnapps
1 teaspoon lemon juice

Batch Recipe (serves 6-8)

1 bottle Champagne
12 ounces orange juice
½ cup peach schnapps
¼ cup fresh lemon juice

Directions

Wash, halve, and squeeze an orange into a measuring pitcher. If desired, strain the juice to filter out pulp and seeds. Combine the peach schnapps and orange juice in a Champagne flute. Tilt the glass to a 45° angle and then slowly add the Champagne until the glass is full.

GLASSWARE: Champagne flute

ORANGE CURE

Ingredients

1 ounce vodka
½ ounce elderflower liqueur
½ ounce pear liqueur
2 ounces fresh squeezed orange juice
5 ounces cuvée

Batch Recipe (serves 10-12)

6 ounces vodka
6 ounces elderflower liqueur
6 ounces pear liqueur
10 ounces orange juice
1 bottle cuvée

Directions

Combine the vodka, elderflower liqueur, and pear liqueur in the glass. Swirl or gently stir to mix. Tilt the glass to a 45° angle and slowly add the cuvée. Top with the orange juice and serve.

GLASSWARE: Champagne flute, wine glass, stemless wine glass

STRAWBELLINI

Ingredients
4-5 ounces Brut
1 ounce gin
¾ ounce strawberry liqueur
Strawberry garnish

Batch Recipe (serves 6-8)
1 bottle Brut
1½ cups gin
1 cup strawberry liqueur
2 cups sliced strawberries to garnish

Directions
Combine the gin and strawberry liqueur in the glass and stir to mix. Tilt the glass
to a 45° angle and slowly add the Brut until the glass is filled to the top. Garnish
with a strawberry.

GLASSWARE: Champagne flute

THE FIRST LADY

Ingredients
1 ½ ounces gin
5 ounces Brut
¾ ounce blueberry simple syrup*
½ ounce limoncello
½ ounce lemon juice
Blueberry garnish

Batch Recipe (serves 8-10)
6 ounces gin
1 bottle Brut
4 ounces blueberry simple syrup*
4 ounces limoncello
3 ounces lemon juice
Blueberry garnish

Directions
Pour the gin, blueberry simple syrup, limoncello, and lemon juice into the glass
and gently swirl or stir. Tilt the glass to a 45° angle and slowly add the Brut.
Garnish with blueberries and serve.

*See the blueberry simple syrup recipe on page 133.

GLASSWARE: stemless wine glass, snifter, bucket glass

SCOTTISH SUN

Ingredients
4 ounces prosecco
2 ounces freshly squeezed clementines
¾ ounce Drambuie

Batch Recipe (serves 6-8)
1 bottle prosecco
4 cups freshly squeezed clementines
(about 2 dozen small)
1 cup Drambuie

Directions
Wash and halve about 2 dozen clementines. Squeeze the juice, then filter for pulp and seeds. Combine the juice with the Drambuie and stir to mix. Tilt the glass to a 45° angle and slowly add the prosecco until the glass is filled to the top.

GLASSWARE: Champagne flute, stemless wine glass

PINK PETTICOAT

Ingredients

4 ounces Champagne

1 ¼ ounces bourbon

1 ounce limoncello

½ cup organic raspberries

½ ounce lemon juice

3 dashes bitters

Batch Recipe (serves 6 - 8)

1 bottle Champagne

1 ½ cups bourbon

1 cup limoncello

1 ½ cups raspberries

¼ cup lemon juice

10 dashes bitters

Directions

Wash and gently dry the raspberries, then muddle them in the bourbon and limoncello. Pour the mixture in batches through the strainer to filter the raspberry seeds and pulp, and use a spoon or spatula to help coax the liquid through. Add the fresh lemon juice, tilt the glass to a 45° angle, and slowly add the Champagne until the glass is full.

GLASSWARE: Champagne flute, stemless wine glass

BECKY BOONE

Ingredients

4-5 ounces Brut
1 ounce bourbon
½ ounce lemon juice
¼ teaspoon Fernet-Branca
Pinch of sugar
Lemon twist garnish

Batch Recipe (serves 10-12)

1 bottle Brut
10 ounces bourbon
2 ounces fresh lemon juice
1 ounce Fernet-Branca
¼ cup sugar
Sliced lemon wheels

Directions

Squeeze 2 ounces of fresh lemon juice (about 2 lemons). Strain the pulp and seeds if desired. Combine with the bourbon and Fernet-Branca in the glass. Tilt the glass to a 45° angle and slowly add the Brut until the glass is filled to the top. Garnish with a lemon twist.

GLASSWARE: Champagne flute, stemless wine glass

FOUNTAIN OF YOUTH

Ingredients
4-5 ounces prosecco
1 ounce gin
2 teaspoons pomegranate juice
2 teaspoons blackberry liqueur
1 teaspoon fresh lemon juice
Lemon wheel garnish

Batch Recipe (serves 8-10)
1 bottle prosecco
8 ounces gin
3 ounces pomegranate juice
3 ounces blackberry liqueur
2 ounces fresh lemon juice
Lemon wheel garnish

Directions
Combine the blackberry liqueur, pomegranate juice, and lemon juice in a Champagne flute. Tilt the glass to a 45° angle and then slowly add the Champagne until the glass is full. Garnish with a lemon wheel.

GLASSWARE: Champagne flute, stemless wine glass

THE DOSIE-DO

Ingredients
4-5 ounces Champagne
1½ ounces fresh grapefruit juice
1 ounce pomegranate vodka

Batch Recipe (serves 6-8)
1 bottle Champagne
2 cups fresh grapefruit juice
1½ cups pomegranate vodka
Thinly sliced grapefruit wheels
and pomegranate seeds garnish

Directions
Wash, halve, and squeeze a grapefruit into a measuring pitcher. If desired, strain
the juice to filter out pulp and seeds. Add 1½ ounces of the fresh grapefruit juice
to a Champagne flute, followed by 1 ounce of pomegranate vodka. Tilt the glass
to a 45° angle and slowly add the Champagne until the glass is filled to the top.

GLASSWARE: Champagne flute, stemless wine glass

THE REDHEAD

Ingredients

2 ounces Irish whiskey

4 ounces pure carrot juice

½ ounce beet shrub*

5 dashes Tabasco® sauce

Lemon wedge garnish

Batch Recipe (serves 4-6)

8 ounces Irish whiskey

20 ounces pure carrot juice

2 ounces beet shrub*

1 teaspoon Tabasco® sauce

Lemon garnish

Directions

Strain the beet shrub to filter out the beets and combine the liquid with the carrot juice. Mix well. Pour the mixture into a martini shaker filled with ice, then add the Irish whiskey and Tabasco® sauce. Shake several times to mix and chill, then strain into a glass filled with ice. Garnish with a wedge of lemon and serve.

*See the beet shrub recipe on page 135.

GLASSWARE: lowball, bucket glass, highball

THE NATURAL

Ingredients

2 ounces vodka
1 large kale leaf
3 ounces homemade lemonade
½ cup blueberries
Kale garnish
Blueberry garnish

Batch Recipe (serves 8-10)

1 750 ml bottle vodka
1 bushel kale
40 ounces homemade lemonade
12 ounces blueberries
Kale garnish
Blueberry garnish

Directions

Muddle the kale in the vodka until the vodka begins to turn green and the kale starts to break apart. To collect the kale pieces, filter the vodka through a strainer and into a martini shaker. Add the blueberries to the vodka and muddle until the blueberries break apart. Filter again to strain out the blueberry pieces. Fill a shaker with ice and add the vodka mixture and lemonade. Shake to mix and chill, then strain into a glass filled with ice. Garnish with kale and blueberries.

GLASSWARE: lowball, bucket glass, highball

THE LIONESS

Ingredients

1 ½ ounces gin
3 ounces freshly squeezed grapefruit juice
3-4 dashes orange bitters
Himalayan salt for the rim

Batch Recipe (serves 8-10)

15 ounces gin
1.76 liters grapefruit juice
2 ounces orange bitters

Directions

Fill a martini shaker with ice and add the gin, grapefruit juice, and orange bitters.
Shake a few times to mix and chill. Run a slice of grapefruit around the rim of the
glass, then dip the rim into a thin layer of Himalayan salt. Shake off the excess.
Fill the glass with ice, then strain the cocktail into the glass.

GLASSWARE: lowball, bucket glass, highball, stemless wine glass

CALI BRUNCH

Ingredients

2 ounces vodka
1 cup tomato juice
1 ounce California black olive juice
1 teaspoon horseradish
¼ teaspoon Tabasco® sauce
1 tablespoon Worcestershire sauce
½ ounce fresh lemon juice
1 cup tomato juice
4 California black olives garnish
Garnishes: dilly beans, pickled carrots,
California black olives, and lemon

Cali Brunch Batch (serves 12-15)

12-20 ounces vodka to taste
56 ounces tomato juice
3 ounces lemon juice
2½ tablespoons horseradish
2 ounces Worcestershire sauce
1 tablespoon Tabasco® sauce
½ teaspoon salt
1 tablespoon ground pepper

Directions

In a large measuring pitcher or mixing bowl, combine the California black olive juice, horseradish, Tabasco® sauce, Worcestershire sauce, and lemon juice. Mix the ingredients together until the horseradish is smooth. Add the tomato juice, salt, and pepper to taste, stirring well. Fill your glass with ice and add your desired amount of vodka, followed by the Bloody Mary mix. Stir. then garnish.

GLASSWARE: highball, pint glass

THE DIRTY GHERKIN

Ingredients

3 ounces vodka
¾ ounce gherkin juice
½ ounce dry vermouth
3 dashes lemon bitters
Gherkin garnish
Lemon garnish (optional)

Directions

Fill a martini shaker with ice. Add the vodka, gherkin juice, dry vermouth, and lemon bitters. Shake to mix and chill, then strain into a martini glass. Garnish with a gherkin and lemon wedge and serve.

GLASSWARE: martini glass, rocks glass

FREDA'S MARTINI

Ingredients

3 ounces vodka

1 ounce California black olive juice

¼ teaspoon dry vermouth

3 California black olives

Directions

Fill a martini shaker with ice. Add the vodka, black olive juice, and dry vermouth. Shake for several seconds to mix, then strain into a martini glass. Garnish with black olives and serve.

GLASSWARE: martini glass

BACK PORCH BEER

Ingredients
1 ½ ounces Patrón Silver
5 ounces Mexican beer
½ ounce lime juice
¼ ounce California black olive juice
¼ ounce homemade sweet and sour*
Pinch of pico de gallo
California black olive garnish

Directions
In a shaker filled with ice, combine the tequila, lime juice, California olive juice, sweet and sour, and pico de gallo. Shake for several seconds until well mixed. Strain into a chilled glass and add the beer. Garnish with California black olives.

*See the homemade sweet and sour recipe on page 133.

GLASSWARE: stemless wine glass, snifter, bucket glass

BEER GARDEN

Ingredients

2 ounces gin

1 ounce triple sec

½ cup organic blackberries

8 ounces pale ale

1 inch fresh rosemary

Blackberry garnish

Directions

In a measuring pitcher or pint glass, muddle the rosemary, blackberries, and gin until the blackberries have broken apart and released all of their juices. Strain the mixture into a martini shaker to filter out the blackberries and rosemary. Add ice to the shaker and shake for a few seconds to chill. Strain into the glass and add the pale ale. Garnish with blackberries and serve.

GLASSWARE: pint glass, highball, bucket glass

KENTUCKY FLAMETHROWER

Ingredients
2½ ounces bourbon
10 ounces dark beer
3 ounces orange juice
1 jalapeño slice
Orange garnish

Directions
In a measuring pitcher or pint glass, combine the bourbon and jalapeño slice. Press the jalapeño slice a few times to release the flavor. Strain into martini shaker and add the orange juice. Stir well. Pour the mixture into the glass and add the beer. Garnish with a slice of orange and serve.

GLASSWARE: pint glass, highball, bucket glass

RASPBERRY ALE

Ingredients
2½ ounces pepper vodka
1½ ounce lemon juice
¼ teaspoon Tabasco® sauce
1 ounce raspberry simple syrup*
1 bottle Mexican beer
Raspberry garnish

Directions
Combine the pepper vodka, lemon juice, Tabasco® sauce, and raspberry simple
syrup in a martini shaker with ice. Shake a few times to chill, then strain into the
glass. Slowly add the beer, stopping every few ounces to avoid overflow.
Garnish with raspberries and serve.

*See the raspberry simple syrup recipe on page 133.

GLASSWARE: pint glass, highball, bucket glass

ISLAND ZEPHYR

Ingredients (serves 2)
2 cups frozen pineapples
1 cup ice
2½ ounces coconut rum
1½ ounces coconut juice
2 ounces banana liqueur
½ ounce fresh lime juice
Lime wheel garnish

Directions
Put the frozen pineapples into a blender along with the coconut rum, coconut juice, banana liqueur, and lime juice. Blend to the desired consistency and garnish with a slice of lime.

GLASSWARE: stemless wine glass, bucket glass, snifter

BANANA COLADA

Ingredients (serves 2)
1½ ounces dark rum
1½ ounces light rum
1 ounce banana liqueur
1 frozen ripe banana
½ ounce coconut cream fat
2 cups frozen pineapple juice cubes
Roasted pineapple chunk garnish

Batch Recipe (serves 6)
8 ounces dark rum
8 ounces light rum
5 ounces banana liqueur
3 frozen ripe bananas
2 ounces coconut cream fat
4 cups frozen pineapple juice cubes
2 cups ice cubes (to add bulk)
Roasted pineapple chunk garnish

Directions
Combine the dark rum, light rum, banana liqueur, frozen ripe bananas, coconut cream fat, frozen pineapple juice cubes, and ice in a blender. Blend until smooth. For a thicker consistency, add more ice. For a thinner consistency, add rum or water. Serve with a roasted pineapple garnish.

GLASSWARE: highball, snifter

FROZEN PINK ICY

Ingredients (serves 4)

6 ounces chilled dragonfruit vodka

1½ chilled vanilla brandy

3 ounces half-and-half

1 can organic frozen pink lemonade

5 cups ice

Directions

In a blender, combine the dragonfruit vodka, vanilla brandy, half-and-half, frozen pink lemonade, and ice. Blend until smooth and serve.

GLASSWARE: stemless wine glass, snifter, highball

GIDDYUP

Ingredients

4 ounces cinnamon whisky

2 ounces Tuaca

½ teaspoon chile cocoa powde

15 frozen horchata cubes*

Directions

In a blender, combine the cinnamon whisky, Tuaca, chile cocoa powder, and horchata cubes. Blend until smooth and pour into a glass rimmed with the chile cocoa powder blend.

*See the frozen horchata cubes recipe on page 135.

GLASSWARE: lowball, rocks glass

ISLAND AVALANCHE

Ingredients (serves 4)

6 ounces vanilla vodka

2 ounces Tuaca

2 ounces mint simple syrup*

1 ounce half-and-half

3 cups frozen pineapple juice cubes

4 cups frozen coconut water cubes

Sweetened coconut flakes garnish

Directions

In a blender, combine the vanilla vodka, Tuaca, mint simple syrup, half-and-half, frozen pineapple cubes, and frozen coconut water cubes. Blend until smooth. For a thicker consistency, add regular ice. For a thinner consistency, add more vodka or half-and-half. Pour into your glass and garnish with sweetened coconut flakes.

*See the mint simple syrup recipe on page 133.

GLASSWARE: bucket glass, highball, lowball

BAJA CALI COAST SANGRIA

Ingredients (serves 6-8)

1 bottle chilled Chardonnay

1 cup silver tequila

⅔ cup agave liqueur

½ cup orange juice

3 ounces fresh lime juice

1 whole Minneola tangelo, thinly sliced

1 whole lemon, thinly sliced

2 whole limes, chopped

½ cup extra fine baker's sugar

Directions

Combine the Chardonnay, tequila, agave liqueur, orange juice, and sugar in a pitcher. Stir until the sugar has dissolved. Wash and slice or chop the fruit and layer or mix into the wine cocktail. Serve immediately or cover and store in a cool, shaded place for up to 24 hours. Refrigerate for up to 10 days.

GLASSWARE: pitcher or punch bowl

CITRUS SANGRIA

Ingredients (serves 6-8)

1 bottle Cabernet Sauvignon

1 cup grapefruit liqueur

½ cup triple sec

⅓ cup ultra fine baker's sugar

2 sliced grapefruits

2 sliced oranges

2 sliced lemons

2 sliced limes

Directions

Combine the Cabernet Sauvignon, grapefruit liqueur, triple sec, and sugar
in a pitcher. Stir until the sugar has dissolved. Wash and slice or chop the fruit
and layer or mix into the wine cocktail. Serve immediately or cover and store
in a cool, shaded place for up to 24 hours. Refrigerate for up to 10 days.

GLASSWARE: pitcher, punch bowl

MULLED WINE

Ingredients (serves 6-8)

1 bottle of red wine
3 cups plain apple cider
2 large oranges
1 cup brandy
¼ cup honey
¼ cup lemon juice
1 teaspoon allspice
1 teaspoon cinnamon
1 teaspoon ground cloves
10 whole cloves
Star anise garnish

Directions

In a large pitcher, measure 3 cups of apple cider and 1 cup of brandy. Slowly pour in the red wine and stir in the ingredients to mix. Add the allspice, cinnamon, ground cloves, whole cloves, whole cinnamon, and star anise to the mixture. Soften the honey by immersing the honey bottle in a bowl of hot water. Add the honey to the pitcher. Add the lemon juice and the orange zest. Stir the wine mixture well, cover it, and set it aside for 2-24 hours. To serve, filter the wine through a fine strainer. Garnish with star anise.

GLASSWARE: wine glasses or stemless wine glasses

STAR-SPANGLED SANGRIA

Ingredients (serves 6-8)
1 bottle chilled Chardonnay
1 cup peach schnapps
½ cup vanilla brandy
½ cup extra fine baker's sugar
2 cups strawberries
2 apples
2 cups blueberries
1 lemon (for apple slice preservation)
Star-shaped cookie cutter

Directions
Combine the Chardonnay, peach schnapps, vanilla brandy, and sugar in a pitcher or punch bowl and stir until the sugar dissolves. Wash the blueberries and set aside. Wash the strawberries, remove the tops, slice, and set aside. Wash the apples and thinly slice lengthwise. Store the slices in a bowl of lemon water to keep them from browning as you work. Use the star-shaped cookie cutter to punch out apple stars. Return the stars to the lemon water to preserve until use. For a red, white, and blue layered sangria, use a pitcher. Add the strawberries first, followed by the apple stars and the blueberries. Slowly pour in the sangria mix until the pitcher is filled. For a red, white, and blue potpourri, add the fruit directly to the sangria mixture and stir.

GLASSWARE: pitcher, punch bowl

TROPICAL SANGRIA

Ingredients (serves 8-10)

1 bottle chilled Chardonnay

6 ounces pineapple juice

¾ cup white rum

¾ cup mango simple syrup*

⅔ cup banana schnapps

⅓ cup lychee liqueur

1 ounce fresh lime juice

1 ripe pineapple

7 kiwis

Directions

In a large pitcher or punch bowl, combine the Chardonnay, pineapple juice, rum, mango simple syrup, banana schnapps, lychee liqueur, and fresh lime juice. Stir to mix. Remove the skin of the pineapple, chop, and add to the wine cocktail. Peel the kiwis, slice horizontally, and add to the wine cocktail. Note that if the kiwis are very ripe, they will begin to break down quickly. Consider waiting until you intend to serve the sangria to add the kiwi, or, if desired, filter the cocktail before serving to collect the fruit's debris. Serve immediately or cover and store in a cool, shaded place for up to 24 hours. Refrigerate for up to 10 days.

*See the mango simple syrup recipe on page 133.

GLASSWARE: pitcher, punch bowl

THE FLIRT

Ingredients

1½ ounces vodka

½ ounce orange brandy liqueur

1½ ounces homemade lemonade

1 ounce cranberry juice

Dash lemon bitters (optional)

½ inch sprig rosemary

Pinch of orange zest

Lemon wedge garnish

Rosemary sprig garnish

Batch Recipe (serves 10-12)

1 bottle vodka

6 ounces orange brandy liqueur

25 ounces homemade lemonade with orange zest

15 ounces cranberry juice

1½ ounces lemon bitters (optional)

Lemon wheel garnish

Rosemary sprig garnish

Directions

Combine the fresh rosemary and vodka in a martini shaker and gently muddle the rosemary to release the flavor. To collect the rosemary pieces, filter the vodka through a strainer and into a shaker filled with ice. Add the lemonade, cranberry juice, orange brandy liqueur, orange zest, and lemon bitters. Shake to mix and chill, then strain into a martini glass or glass filled with ice. Garnish with a lemon wedge and rosemary sprig.

GLASSWARE: lowball, highball, bucket glass, stemless wine glass

GIN MOJITO

Ingredients
2 ounces gin
¾ ounce lime juice
¾ ounce mint simple syrup*
2 ounces club soda
Fresh mint garnish

Directions
In a martini shaker filled with ice, combine the gin, lime juice, and mint simple syrup. Shake several times to mix and chill. Strain the mixture into a glass filled with ice. Top with club soda and stir. Garnish with a mint sprig.

*See the mint simple syrup recipe on page 133.

GLASSWARE: lowball, rocks glass, bucket glass, stemless wine glass

BANANA BEACH

Ingredients

1 ½ ounces white rum

¾ ounce banana liqueur

1 ounce pineapple juice

1 ounce orange juice

1 tablespoon lime juice

1 teaspoon maraschino cherry syrup

Slice of orange for garnish

Cocktail cherry garnish*

Batch Recipe (serves 8-10)

10 ounces white rum

3 ounces banana liqueur

12 ounces pineapple juice

4 ounces orange juice

2 ounces lime juice

1 ½ ounces maraschino cherry syrup

1 whole pineapple, sliced

2 oranges, sliced

Cocktail cherry garnish*

Directions

Fill a martini shaker with ice. Combine the rum, pineapple juice, orange juice, banana liqueur, maraschino cherry syrup, and lime juice, and shake several times to mix and chill. Strain into a glass filled with ice, or into a martini glass. Garnish with cocktail cherries and orange slices.

*See the homemade maraschino recipe on page 135.

GLASSWARE: rocks, lowball, bucket glass, highball, stemless wine glass

BLACK RUBY

Ingredients

2 ounces tequila
⅓ cup blackberries
5 mint leaves
¾ ounce orange liqueur
2 ounces homemade sweet and sour*
Mint sprig and lime wedge garnish
Salted or sugared rim

Batch Recipe (serves 10-12)

1 bottle (750ml) tequila
2 packages blackberries
1 package mint
1 cup orange liqueur
10 ounces homemade sweet and sour*
Mint and lime garnish
Salted or sugared rim

Directions

In a measuring pitcher or large glass, muddle the blackberries until most of the berries have been crushed and a small amount of juice is present. Pour the mixture through a filter to strain out the pulp and seeds. In a new measuring pitcher, muddle the mint in the tequila until the tequila begins to turn green or you've reached your desired amount of mint flavoring. To catch the mint pieces, strain the mint tequila mixture as you add it to the blackberry juice. Fill a martini shaker with ice. Add the orange liqueur, homemade sweet and sour, and blackberry mint tequila combination. Shake for several seconds to mix and chill. Strain into a glass packed with ice and garnish with a fresh sprig of mint and lime wedge.

*See the homemade sweet and sour recipe on page 133.

GLASSWARE: bucket glass, lowball, rocks glass

GOOD-LUCK CHARM

Ingredients

2 ounces lemon vodka

2 ounces pineapple juice

½ ounce homemade sweet and sour*

½ ounce mint simple syrup*

2 ounces club soda (optional)

Mint sprig and lemon wedge garnish

Directions

Fill a martini shaker with ice, then add the lemon vodka, pineapple juice, homemade simple syrup, and mint simple syrup. Shake several times to mix and chill, then strain into a glass filled with ice or into a martini glass. If you've added club soda to your drink, pour your drink into an empty shaker and then back into your glass. Garnish with a fresh sprig of mint and lemon wedge.

*See the homemade sweet and sour and mint simple syrup recipes on page 133.

GLASSWARE: bucket glass, highball, stemless wine glass

CARIBBEAN CURSE

Ingredients

1 cup homemade horchata*

2 ounces dark rum

1 ounce amaretto

Cinnamon stick and dusting of ground cinnamon for garnish

Horchata Cocktail Batch (Serves 6-8)

24 ounces homemade horchata*

7 ounces dark rum

3 ounces amaretto

Directions

Combine the horchata, dark rum, and amaretto in a martini shaker with ice. Shake for a few seconds to mix and chill. Strain into a glass filled with ice. Garnish with a cinnamon stick and a dusting of ground cinnamon.

*See the homemade horchata recipe on page 135.

GLASSWARE: highball, bucket glass, wine glass

HEARTTHROB

Ingredients

1 ounce vodka
1 ounce blackberry liqueur
½ ounce orange liqueur
½ ounce fresh lime juice
1½ ounces lemonade
1½ ounces pomegranate juice
Fresh blackberry garnish

Batch Recipe (serves 10-12)

6 ounces vodka
4 ounces blackberry liqueur
3 ounces orange liqueur
2 ounces fresh lime juice
15 ounces lemonade
12 ounces pomegranate juice
1 cup blackberry garnishes for individual glasses
2 oranges thinly sliced into wheels
1 lemon thinly sliced into wheels

Directions

Fill a martini shaker with ice. Combine the vodka, blackberry liqueur, orange liqueur, lime juice, lemonade, and pomegranate juice in the shaker and shake for several seconds to mix. Strain into a glass filled with ice or into a martini glass. Garnish with blackberries and serve.

GLASSWARE: lowball, bucket, rocks glass, martini glass

JULIE'S SELTZER WATER

Ingredients

1½ ounces vodka
1 ounce pomegranate juice
1 ounce lemonade
½ ounce fresh lime juice
2 ounces tonic water
Lime garnish

Batch Recipe (serves 10-12)

10 ounces vodka
12 ounces pomegranate juice
12 ounces lemonade
4 ounces fresh lime juice
10 ounces tonic water
5 limes thinly sliced into wheels

Directions

Fill a martini shaker with ice and add the vodka, pomegranate juice, lemonade, and lime juice. Shake for several seconds to mix. Strain into a glass filled with ice, then empty the shaker. Slowly add 2 ounces of tonic water. Stir the drink to mix or pour into the shaker and back into the glass. Garnish with lime wheels.

GLASSWARE: lowball, rocks glass, bucket glass

CACHAÇA LEMONGRASS

Ingredients

2 ounces cachaça
3 ounces pineapple juice
¾ ounce banana schnapps
½ ounce lime juice
¼ teaspoon ginger juice
1 stalk lemongrass

Batch Recipe (serves 10-12)

16 ounces cachaça
30 ounces pineapple juice
6 ounces banana schnapps
2 ounces lime juice
2 teaspoons ginger juice
2 stalks lemongrass

Directions

Peel two to three outer layers of lemongrass leaves away and toss. Cut the stalks into three or four pieces and add to a shaker or measuring pitcher. Add the cachaça and muddle until the lemongrass begins to break apart. To collect the lemongrass pieces, strain the cachaça into a martini shaker. To make the ginger juice, peel and thinly slice the ginger piece. Use a garlic press to collect the ginger juice and add it to the cachaça. Add the pineapple juice and banana schnapps, then fill the shaker with ice. Shake to mix and chill, and strain into your glass. Garnish with lemongrass and ginger.

GLASSWARE: rocks glass, bucket glass, highball

THE SEÑORITA

Ingredients
3 ounces homemade horchata*
1 ounce chocolate coffee tequila-based liqueur
½ ounce orange brandy
Chocolate shavings
Cinnamon stick garnish

Batch Recipe (serves 6-8)
24 ounces homemade horchata*
7 ounces chocolate coffee tequila-based liqueur
3 ounces orange brandy
6 cinnamon sticks for garnish

Directions
Fill a martini shaker with ice and add the horchata, chocolate coffee tequila-based liqueur, and orange brandy. Shake for several seconds to chill and mix. Strain into a glass filled with ice and garnish with chocolate shavings and a cinnamon stick.

*See the homemade horchata recipe on page 135.

GLASSWARE: lowball, bucket glass, rocks glass, snifter, stemless wine glass

MARTA'S MULBERRY MADNESS

Ingredients

½ cup fresh mulberries or 2 ounces mulberry juice

1 ½ ounces white rum

1 ounce pineapple juice

¾ ounce clear orange liqueur

2 ounces blood orange soda

Garnish with fresh mulberries

Batch Recipe (serves 8-10)

3 cups fresh mulberries or 1 cup mulberry juice

2 cups white rum

2 cups pineapple juice

½ cup clear orange liqueur

3 cups blood orange soda

Garnish with fresh mulberries

Directions

Wash the mulberries, then muddle them in a measuring pitcher or pint glass until all the berries are crushed. To remove the pulp and stems, filter through a fine strainer or squeeze through a cheesecloth and into a mixing bowl or measuring pitcher. Once the maximum amount of juice has been collected, pour the juice into a martini shaker. Add the rum, pineapple juice, and orange liqueur to the shaker. Fill the shaker with ice and shake for several seconds to mix and chill. Strain into a glass packed with ice or serve neat. Garnish with fresh mulberries.

GLASSWARE: bucket glass, stemless wine glass

THE MILANO

Ingredients

2 ounces gin

5 ounces Italian orange soda

¼ elderflower liqueur

¼ triple sec

½ ounce fresh lime juice

Orange slice garnish

Batch Recipe (serves 15-18)

16 ounces gin

42 ounces Italian orange soda

4 ounces elderflower liqueur

4 ounces triple sec

4 ounces fresh lime juice

3 oranges thinly sliced into wheels

Directions

Fill a martini shaker with ice. Add the gin, Italian orange soda, elderflower liqueur, triple sec, and fresh lime juice and shake a few times to mix and chill. Strain into a glass filled with ice and garnish with a slice of orange.

GLASSWARE: bucket glass, lowball, stemless wine glass

THE DOROSENCO

Ingredients

1 ½ ounces pink lemon juice
1 ounce water
1 ounce sugar
2 ounces white rum
¾ ounce clear orange liqueur
Pink lemon wedge garnish

Batch Recipe (serves 6-8)

32 pink lemons (1 ¾ cup pink lemon juice)
1 ¾ cups water
1 ½ cups sugar
2 cups white rum
1 cup clear orange liqueur
Pink lemon wedge garnish

Directions

Squeeze 2-3 pink lemons and filter the juice for pulp and seeds. Pour the juice into a martini shaker and add the water and sugar. Stir until the sugar dissolves. Add the rum and orange liqueur into the shaker and stir well. Strain the cocktail into a glass filled with ice and garnish with pink lemon wedges.

GLASSWARE: lowball, bucket glass, stemless wine glass

THE SOPHISTICATE

Ingredients

2 ounces pomegranate vodka
2 ounces cranberry juice
½ ounce triple sec
¼ ounce orange juice
¼ ounce fresh lime juice
6 mint leaves
Pinch of orange zest
Mint leaf garnish
Whole cranberry garnish

Batch Recipe (serves 8-10)

2 cups pomegranate vodka
4 cups cranberry juice
½ cup triple sec
½ cup orange juice
¼ cup fresh lime juice
4 mint sprigs
2 tablespoons orange zest
Mint leaf garnish
Whole cranberry garnish

Directions

Wash and pat dry the mint, then drop it into a large measuring pitcher or mixing bowl. Add the pomegranate vodka and muddle the mint until the vodka develops a faint green hue. Filter the mint and vodka mixture through a strainer and into a martini shaker filled with ice. Add the cranberry juice, triple sec, orange juice, lime juice, and orange zest. Shake well to mix and chill, then strain into a martini glass. Garnish with mint leaves and whole cranberries.

GLASSWARE: martini glass

PROMISCUOUS PEACH

Ingredients

1½ ounces white rum

1½ ounces peach nectar

¾ ounce peach schnapps

3 ounces homemade lemonade

Sliced lemon garnish

Sliced peach garnish

Batch Recipe (serves 10-12)

1 bottle white rum

12 ounces peach nectar

6 ounces peach schnapps

25 ounces homemade lemonade

Sliced lemons for garnish

Sliced peaches for garnish

Directions

Fill a martini shaker with ice. Add the white rum, peach nectar, peach schnapps, and homemade lemonade. Shake to mix and chill, then strain into a glass filled with ice. Garnish with lemons and peaches and serve.

GLASSWARE: lowball, highball, bucket glass

THIS GIRL'S MINT JULEP

Ingredients
3 ounces bourbon
1 ounce mint simple syrup*
Sprig of mint leaves garnish
Crushed ice

Directions
Wrap two cups of crushed ice in kitchen towels and pound with a meat tenderizer
or a rolling pin until the ice is finely smashed. Scoop the ice into a silver cup,
then add the mint simple syrup, followed by the bourbon. Garnish with a fresh
sprig of mint and serve.

*See the mint simple syrup recipe on page 133.

GLASSWARE: lowball, highball, bucket glass

THE DAISY MAE

Ingredients

2 ounces vodka

½ ounce triple sec

½ ounce lemon juice

1 cup watermelon cubes

3 basil leaves

2 ounces soda water (optional)

Watermelon balls garnish

Batch Recipe (serves 8-10)

4 cups vodka

¾ cup triple sec

½ cup fresh lemon juice

1 large watermelon, juiced

1 small package basil

2 10-ounce bottles soda water (optional)

Directions

Muddle the basil leaves in the vodka, then strain to filter out the vodka and set aside.
Muddle the watermelon or use a food processor to collect the watermelon juice.
Fill a martini shaker with ice and add the vodka with basil, watermelon juice, triple
sec, and lemon juice. Shake well to mix and chill, then strain into a martini glass
or a bucket glass filled with ice. Garnish with basil leaves and watermelon balls.

GLASSWARE: martini glass, lowball, bucket glass

AFTERNOON DELIGHT

Ingredients

2 ounces clear corn whiskey
2 ounces homemade sweet and sour*
1 ½ ounces cranberry juice
½ ounce mint simple syrup*
Whole cranberries for garnish
Fresh mint garnish

Batch Recipe (serves 10-12)

25 ounces clear corn whiskey
10 ounces homemade sweet and sour*
15 ounces cranberry juice
4 ounces mint simple syrup*
Whole cranberries for garnish
Fresh mint garnish

Directions

Fill a martini shaker with ice. Combine the clear corn whiskey, homemade sweet and sour, cranberry juice, and mint simple syrup in the shaker and shake several times until mixed and chilled. Strain into a glass filled with ice or a martini glass. Garnish with a sprig of mint and a few whole cranberries.

*See homemade sweet and sour and mint simple syrup recipes on page 133.

GLASSWARE: rocks glass, bucket glass, lowball, martini glass

THE SOMBRERO

Ingredients

1½ ounces chocolate coffee tequila-based liqueur

3 ounces chocolate almond milk

½ ounce orange-flavored cognac

Pinch cocoa chile blend powder

Pinch orange zest

Chocolate shavings for garnish

Orange zest garnish

Batch Recipe (serves 10-12)

12ounces chocolate coffee tequila-based liqueur

1 carton chocolate almond milk

5 ounces orange-flavored cognac

1 tablespoon cocoa chile blend powder

1 tablespoon orange zest

Chocolate shavings for garnish

Orange zest garnish

Directions

In a martini shaker, combine the chocolate coffee tequila-based liqueur, chocolate almond milk, orange-flavored cognac, cocoa chile blend powder, and orange zest. Mix well until cocoa chile blend powder has dissolved. Add ice to the shaker and shake several times to chill. Strain into a glass filled with ice and garnish with orange zest and chocolate shavings.

GLASSWARE: highball, pint glass, bucket glass

SLEEPING BEAUTY

Ingredients

1 ounce rum-based coffee liqueur

4-5 ounces hot decaf coffee

½ ounce warmed half and half

¾ ounce blackberry liqueur

¾ ounce orange cinnamon simple syrup*

Chocolate shavings for garnish

Blackberries for garnish

Directions

Brew a small batch of fresh decaf coffee. Pour four to five ounces into your cup
followed by the warmed half and half, blackberry liqueur, and orange cinnamon
simple syrup. Gently stir to mix. Top with whipped cream, fresh blackberries,
and chocolate shavings.

*See orange cinnamon simple syrup recipe on page 133.

GLASSWARE: coffee mug, teacup

TEA PARTY

Ingredients

3 ounces tea-infused vodka
½ ounce orange clove simple syrup*
¼ ounce mint simple syrup*
¼ ounce lemon juice
2 ounces club soda (optional)
Lemon and mint garnish

Batch Recipe (serves 8-10)

1 bottle tea-infused vodka (3-5 bags of tea)
¾ cup orange clove simple syrup*
½ cup mint simple syrup*
½ cup lemon juice
20 ounces club soda

Directions

Fill a martini shaker with ice, and add the tea-infused vodka, orange clove simple syrup, mint simple syrup, and lemon juice. Shake to mix and chill, then strain into a glass and serve. Garnish with mint and lemon.

Tea-Infused Vodka

To make tea-infused vodka, soak a bag of tea in 6 ounces of vodka for 1 to 24 hours depending on your desired strength of tea. Filter the vodka through a strainer to collect the teabags. Store in a sealable container for up to 10 days or use immediately.

*See mint and orange clove simple syrup recipes on page 133.

GLASSWARE: highball, martini glass

HOT AND SWEET

Ingredients

4 ounces vodka
½ cup chopped cucumber
½ ounce lime juice
2 ounces pineapple juice
¹⁄₁₆ teaspoon cayenne pepper
1 ounce agave syrup
Cayenne pepper rim (optional)

Batch Recipe (serves 6-8)

12 ounces vodka
1 large cucumber, chopped
1½ ounces lime juice
8 ounces pineapple juice
1 teaspoon cayenne pepper
2 ounces agave syrup
Thin cucumber wheels to garnish

Directions

In a measuring pitcher or shaker, muddle the cucumber and cayenne pepper in the vodka until the vodka takes on a light green hue. To filter the cucumber out of the vodka, pour the mixture through a strainer and into a martini shaker. Add the lime juice, pineapple juice, and agave syrup and stir until the agave syrup has dissolved. Add ice to the shaker and shake for several seconds to chill. Strain into the glass and serve.

Optional

To rim the glass with cayenne paper, run a freshly cut lime around the rim of your glass. Next, dip the rim into a plate dusted with cayenne pepper. To shake off the excess, hold the glass over the sink and tap on the body of the glass until the loose pepper stops falling.

GLASSWARE: martini glass, wine glass

FIRE AND ICE

Ingredients (serves 4)

6 ounces tequila reposado

3 ounces orange liqueur

1 ounce fresh lime juice

1 can organic frozen orange juice

1 cup frozen lemonade ice cubes

4 cups ice cubes

1 jalapeño

Lime wheel garnish

Directions

Wash the jalapeño, then slice one to two thin wheels with seeds. In a measuring pitcher, combine the tequila reposado with the jalapeño and gently press the jalapeño with a muddler or the tip of a wooden spoon. You only need to press the seeds once or twice to release a lot of flavor and heat. To remove the jalapeño, filter the tequila reposado through a strainer and into a blender. Add the orange liqueur, frozen orange juice, frozen lemonade ice cubes, and plain ice cubes. Blend until smooth. Garnish with a wheel of lime and serve.

GLASSWARE: snifter, stemless wine glass, bucket glass

SQUARE DANCE

Ingredients

1½ ounces gin
1½ ounces fresh grapefruit juice
½ ounce sloe gin
1 teaspoon honey
2-3 dashes Tabasco® Raspberry Chipotle Sauce
3 basil leaves
Basil leaf garnish

Batch Recipe (serves 8-10)

16 ounces gin
16 ounces fresh grapefruit juice
5 ounces sloe gin
¼ cup honey
2 ounces Tabasco® Raspberry Chipotle Sauce
1 cup basil leaves

Directions

Wash and dry the basil. Combine the basil and gin in a shaker or measuring pitcher and muddle until the gin takes on a slightly green hue. Filter the gin through a strainer into a martini shaker filled with ice. Add the fresh grapefruit juice, sloe gin, honey, and Tabasco® Raspberry Chipotle Sauce to the shaker and shake a few times to mix well and chill. Strain into your glass and garnish with basil.

GLASSWARE: stemless wine glass, lowball, rocks glass

SMOKIN' MANGO

Ingredients

3 ounces mango juice
1½ ounces tequila
1 ounce rum
½ ounce lemon juice
1 teaspoon honey
Pinch of smoked paprika
4 medium basil leaves
Basil leaf garnish

Batch Recipe (serves 10-12)

1 carton mango juice
12 ounces tequila
7 ounces rum
3 ounces lemon juice
2 ounces honey
1 teaspoon smoked paprika
1 bushel basil leaves
Basil leaf garnish
Lemon wheel garnish

Directions

Fill a martini shaker with ice and add the mango juice, rum, lemon juice, honey, and smoked paprika. In a measuring pitcher, muddle the basil leaves in the tequila until the tequila turns slightly green. Strain the tequila mixture in the shaker and discard the basil leaves. Shake all of the ingredients to mix and chill. Strain into a glass. Garnish with a basil leaf and a pinch of paprika. Shake to mix and chill, then strain into a glass and serve. Garnish with mint and lemon.

GLASSWARE: lowball, bucket, stemless wine glass

LOLITA

Ingredients

2 cups frozen strawberries
2 ounces triple sec
4 ounces tequila
1 ounce fresh lime juice
¼ ounce Tabasco® Sweet & Spicy Pepper Sauce
Salt for rim of glass
Strawberry garnish

Directions

In a blender, combine the strawberries, triple sec, tequila, fresh lime juice, and Tabasco® Sweet & Spicy Pepper Sauce. Blend until smooth. Run a lime around the rim of the glass and dip glass into the salt to coat. Pour the cocktail into the glass, garnish with a strawberry, and serve.

GLASSWARE: highball, pint glass, bucket glass

NOVEMBER DREAM

Ingredients

2 ounces bourbon

1½ ounces organic apple cider

¾ ounce cinnamon clove brown sugar simple syrup*

2 teaspoons orange brandy liqueur

1 tablespoon orange juice

Brown sugar for rim (optional)

Punch Recipe (serves 10-12)

1 bottle bourbon

54 ounces organic apple cider

10 ounces cinnamon clove brown sugar simple syrup*

8 ounces orange brandy liqueur

1 tablespoon orange juice

Cloves, cinnamon sticks, and orange wheels for garnish

Directions ~ Martini

Combine the bourbon, apple cider, cinnamon clove brown sugar simple syrup, orange brandy liqueur, and orange juice in a martini shaker. Mix well with a whisk or martini stir stick. Fill the shaker with ice and shake for several seconds to chill. Strain into martini glass and serve.

Directions ~ Punch

About 20 minutes before your guests arrives, combine the apple cider, cinnamon clove brown sugar simple syrup, and orange juice in a crock pot or saucepan. Heat on medium heat. Once your guests arrive, add the bourbon and orange brandy liqueur to the mix. Garnish with cloves, cinnamon sticks, and orange wheels.

*See cinnamon clove brown sugar simple syrup recipe on page 133.

GLASSWARE: stemless wine glass, snifter, bucket glass

EVENING GLORY

Ingredients - Cocktail

2 small scoops pomegranate blueberry sorbet
2 ounces prosecco
¾ ounce orange brandy
½ ounce lemon juice
Pomegranate garnish

Ingredients - Dessert

3 large scoops pomegranate blueberry sorbet
2 ounces prosecco
¾ ounce orange brandy
½ ounce lemon juice
Pomegranate garnish

Directions

Scoop the pomegranate blueberry sorbet into the glass. Pour in the orange brandy, followed by the lemon juice. Top off with well-chilled prosecco. Garnish with fresh pomegranate seeds and serve with spoon or a straw.

GLASSWARE: stemless wine glass, snifter, bucket glass

GIN MINT COOKIE

Ingredients
1 ½ ounces gin
¾ ounce elderflower liqueur
2 ounces fresh grapefruit juice
½ ounce mint simple syrup*
1 thin slice of ginger
2 ounces soda water
Mint sprig garnish
Grapefruit slice garnish

Directions
Peel and slice a thin piece of fresh ginger and add it to a measuring pitcher.
Add the gin to the ginger and, using a muddler or the tip of a wooden spoon, press the ginger 2-3 times to release the flavor, or more if you'd like a stronger ginger presence. To collect the ginger, filter the gin through a strainer and into a martini shaker. Add the fresh grapefruit juice, mint simple syrup, and elderflower liqueur into the shaker and shake for several seconds to mix. Strain into a glass filled with ice and top with soda water. Garnish with fresh mint and a slice of grapefruit.

*See mint simple syrup recipe on page 133.

GLASSWARE: bucket glass, lowball, rocks glass, stemless wine glass

BELLE STARR

Ingredients

2 ounces apple cider
2 ounces pineapple juice
2 ounces spiced rum
½ ounce orange brandy
½ ounce orange clove simple syrup*
¼ ounce brown sugar cinnamon simple syrup*
¼ teaspoon lemon zest
Cinnamon stick and lemon zest garnish

Batch Recipe (serves 12-14)

1 liter apple cider
1 liter pineapple juice
1 bottle spiced rum
12 ounces orange brandy
4 ounces orange clove simple syrup*
3 ounces brown sugar cinnamon simple syrup*
2 tablespoons lemon zest
Cinnamon stick and lemon zest garnish

Directions

In a small saucepan over low heat, combine the apple cider, pineapple juice, spiced rum, orange brandy, orange clove simple syrup, brown sugar simple syrup, and lemon zest. Heat until steam begins to rise from the pan. Remove from the heat and pour into a coffee mug or teacup. Garnish with a cinnamon stick and lemon zest and serve.

*See orange clove and cinnamon clove brown sugar simple syrup recipes on page 133.

GLASSWARE: coffee mug, teacup

SORBET PALOMA

Ingredients - Cocktail
2 small scoops raspberry sorbet
1½ ounces sparkling grapefruit soda
1 ounce tequila
½ ounce orange liqueur
Squeeze of one lime wedge
Wedge of lime and raspberries garnish

Ingredients - Dessert
3 large scoops raspberry sorbet
1½ ounces sparkling grapefruit soda
1 ounce tequila
½ ounce orange liqueur
Squeeze of one lime wedge
Wedge of lime and raspberries garnish

Directions
Add 2 scoops of raspberry sorbet to a lowball or bucket glass. Pour in the tequila, orange liqueur, and lime juice. Slowly add the sparkling grapefruit juice and garnish with a wedge of lime and raspberries.

GLASSWARE: lowball, stemless wine glass, bucket glass

SUNNY SORBET

Ingredients - Cocktail
2 small scoops mango sorbet
1½ ounces coconut rum
1½ ounces pineapple juice
Mango garnish

Ingredients - Dessert
3 large scoops mango sorbet
1½ ounces coconut rum
1½ ounces pineapple juice
Mango garnish

Directions
Scoop the mango sorbet into the glass. Pour in the coconut rum, followed by the pineapple juice. Garnish with a slice of mango and serve with a spoon or a straw.

GLASSWARE: stemless wine glass, snifter, bucket glass

WINNIE PALMER

Ingredients - Cocktail
2 small scoops lemon sorbet
2 ounces chilled black iced tea
¾ ounce blackberry liqueur
¾ ounce lemon vodka
Lemon slice garnish

Ingredients - Dessert
3 large scoops lemon sorbet
2 ounces chilled black iced tea
¾ ounce blackberry liqueur
¾ ounce lemon vodka
Lemon slice garnish

Directions
Add 2 small scoops of lemon sorbet to the glass. Pour in the lemon vodka, blackberry liqueur, and chilled iced tea. Garnish with a slice of lemon.

GLASSWARE: lowball, stemless wine glass, bucket glass

GIN DILL INFUSION

Ingredients (serves 1-4)
1 ½ cups gin
½ cucumber
½ cup dill
½ cup California black olives
Black olive and cucumber garnish

Directions
Peel and slice or chop a cucumber; add it to a sealable container. Strain a half cup of California black olives and add that to the cucumber. Nestle a half cup of dill into the container. Pour in the gin and set aside or refrigerate for two to 24 hours. Every so often, gently shake the container to circulate the cucumber, dill, California black olives, and gin. To serve, measure the desired amount into a martini shaker filled with ice. Shake for several seconds to chill and strain into your glass. Garnish with cucumber and black olives.

GLASSWARE: shot glass, martini glass, rocks glass, bucket

MISSISSIPPI DELTA INFUSION

Ingredients

1 small ripe pineapple
4 inches ginger root
3 mint sprigs
12 ounces bourbon

Directions

Remove the skin, top, and bottom of the pineapple. Slice the pineapple horizontally
to form spears and place them into a large mason jar or sealable pitcher. Peel
about 4 inches of ginger root and slice into thin wheels. Add those pieces to the
pineapple. Wash and dry three small mint sprigs and place inside the jar. Fill the
jar with your favorite bourbon, about 10-16 ounces. Store in a cool shaded spot in
your kitchen or in your refrigerator for 2 to 24 hours. Strain directly into your glass
or strain into a martini shaker filled with ice to shake before serving.

GLASSWARE: martini glass, lowball, rocks glass

SWEET & SOUR

Nothing tastes better than homemade sweet & sour. It will take you 20 minutes to squeeze the citrus, but it's well worth the time spent. Remember, you can always adjust the amount of sugar and water to your liking.

Batch Recipe
2 cups lemon juice
2 cups lime juice
3¾ cups water
3¾ cups sugar

SIMPLE SYRUPS

Simple syrups might seem intimidating to make, but they truly are "simple" and the fastest and easiest way to dress up the most basic cocktails.

Blueberry
1 cup blueberries
1 cup sugar
1 cup water

Raspberry
1 cup raspberries
1 cup sugar
1 cup water

Mango
2 mangos
1 cup sugar
1 cup water

Mint
1 packet mint
1 cup sugar
1 cup water

Cinnamon Clove
3 sticks cinnamon
1 teaspoon whole cloves
1 cup sugar
1 cup water

Orange Clove
1 cup chopped orange
1 teaspoon whole cloves
1 cup sugar
1 cup water

Brown Sugar Cinnamon
1 cup brown sugar
3 cinnamon sticks
1 cup water

MIXERS

Most cocktail mixers taste best after they've had time to sit. When possible, plan to make your mixer a few hours before your guests arrive so that it's ready to go when you need it.

Homemade Horchata

1 cup rice
1 cinnamon stick
1 tablespoon vanilla extract
5 cups water
1 cup vanilla almond milk
½ teaspoon almond extract
¾ cup sugar

Directions

In a pitcher, soak the rice in the water overnight or for 12 hours. Next, add the rest of the ingredients. Stir until the sugar dissolves, then pour the mixture into a blender and blend on high until the rice is pulverized. Strain into a new pitcher and chill until ready for use.

Cocktail Cherry Recipe

2 cups fresh, pitted cherries
2 cups Luxardo liqueur
½ ounce almond extract
½ ounce vanilla extract
¼ ounce orange zest

Directions

Combine all the ingredients in a pitcher and soak for 48 hours before using. Keep covered and refrigerated. Use for two months.

Beet Shrub

1 cup chopped beets
1 cup sugar
1 cup vinegar

Pear Strawberry Rosemary Shrub

2 heaping cups pears
2 heaping cups strawberries
4 4-inch rosemary sprigs
1 cup apple cider vinegar
1 cup sugar

Tangerine Ginger Apple Shrub

1 cup tangerine juice
1 cup red wine vinegar
2 heaping cups apple
⅔ cup ginger
1 cup sugar

ABOUT US

Jordan Catapano

Jordan Catapano, author of *This Girl Walks Into a Bar: A Women's Guide to Professional Bartending and Home Mixology* and *This Girl Minds Her P's & Q's: An Etiquette Handbook for Dinner Parties, Restaurants, and Bars*, has had long experience as a professional bartender and mixologist. She blogs for ThisGirlWalksIntoABar.com and is a mixologist and blogger for BevMo! She has contributed her cocktail expertise to several online sites, including *Self Magazine*, PBS Food, The Huffington Post, *Saveur Magazine*, *The Sacramento Bee*, and *The Bellingham Herald*, and developed cocktail recipes for companies such as Dole®, Tabasco®, Gallo Wine, Patrón Tequila, Dry Soda, Thermador, and Caesarstone. Jordan lives in Los Angeles with her husband and children.

Jocelyn Dunn Muhlbach

Jocelyn Dunn Muhlbach, the graphic designer behind This Girl Walks Into A Bar, created and maintains the company's brand image and produces all artwork for its website, books, and product line. Her background includes work for a wide array of clientele, including Disney, UCLA, USC, BevMo!, Westfield, Princess Cruises, Cal Poly San Luis Obispo, Anne Taintor, E!, Sony Pictures, Pottery Barn, Dreamworks, and Mattel. She lives in Los Angeles with her husband and children.

Jocelyn (left) and Jordan (right)